Family Education for Business-Owning Families

A FAMILY———
BUSINESS
———PUBLICATION

Family Business Publications are the combined efforts of the Family Business Consulting Group and Palgrave Macmillan. These books provide useful information on a broad range of topics that concern the family business enterprise, including succession planning, communication, strategy and growth, family leadership, and more. The books are written by experts with combined experiences of over a century in the field of family enterprise and who have consulted with thousands of enterprising families the world over, giving the reader practical, effective, and time-tested insights to everyone involved in a family business.

FBCG, founded in 1994, is the leading business consultancy exclusively devoted to helping family enterprises prosper across generations.

FAMILY BUSINESS LEADERSHIP SERIES

This series of books comprises concise guides and thoughtful compendiums to the most pressing issues that anyone involved in a family firm may face. Each volume covers a different topic area and provides the answers to some of the most common and challenging questions.

Titles include:

All of the books were written by members of the Family Business Consulting Group and are based on both our experiences with thousands of client families as well as our empirical research at leading research universities the world over.

Family Education for Business-Owning Families

Strengthening Bonds by Learning Together

Amy M. Schuman
and John L. Ward

palgrave
macmillan

FAMILY EDUCATION FOR BUSINESS-OWNING FAMILIES
Copyright © Family Business Consulting Group, 2009, 2011.

All rights reserved.

First published by the Family Business Consulting Group Publications, 2009.

This edition first published in 2011 by
PALGRAVE MACMILLAN®
in the United States—a division of St. Martin's Press LLC,
175 Fifth Avenue, New York, NY 10010.

Where this book is distributed in the UK, Europe and the rest of the world,
this is by Palgrave Macmillan, a division of Macmillan Publishers Limited,
registered in England, company number 785998, of Houndmills,
Basingstoke, Hampshire RG21 6XS.

Palgrave Macmillan is the global academic imprint of the above companies
and has companies and representatives throughout the world.

Palgrave® and Macmillan® are registered trademarks in the United States,
the United Kingdom, Europe and other countries.

ISBN: 978-0-230-11119-6

Library of Congress Cataloging-in-Publication Data

Schuman, Amy M.
    Family education for business-owning families : strengthening
bonds by learning together / by Amy M. Schuman and John L. Ward.
        p. cm. — (Family business leadership series)
    Includes index.
    ISBN 978-0-230-11119-6
        1. Family-owned business enterprises—Management.
    2. Organizational learning. I. Ward, John L., 1945– II. Title.

HD62.25.S368 2011
658.3'124—dc22   2010036089

A catalogue record of the book is available from the British Library.

Design by Newgen Imaging Systems (P) Ltd., Chennai, India.

First Palgrave Macmillan edition: January 2011

10 9 8 7 6 5 4 3 2 1

Printed in the United States of America.

Contents

Exhibits

PART I

FAMILY EDUCATION: THE FAMILY CORE

When moms, dads, grandparents, aunts, uncles, brothers, sisters, cousins, and second cousins learn together, something special takes place. Respect for one another increases. Feelings of family friendship and intimacy are reinvigorated, or perhaps ignited for the first time. Trust builds. People unite. Pride in family grows.

Anything can happen.

Chapter 1

Introduction

The Power of Family Education

Not long before Rupert Murdoch's News Corp. clinched the deal to purchase Dow Jones & Co. and the *Wall Street Journal* from the Bancroft family in 2007, one family member, Crawford Hill, sent an anguished, nearly 4,000-word e-mail to his relatives urging them to accept Murdoch's offer. Family members-owners were "paying the price" for their passivity, which dated back a quarter of a century, he said.

In his letter, Hill recalled that neither his mother nor his grandmother, the family matriarch, "ever spoke of the legacy of Dow Jones, much less the possibility of actually working there or what it meant to be a steward of the business. There was no effort whatsoever at promoting legacy or educating the next generation." He and his grandmother shared a love of biology, but when as a young man he accepted an offer to teach biology at the Episcopal Academy in Philadelphia, she stunned him by saying how disappointed she was that he was not going to join the family business. "We talked about everything under the sun...but never Dow Jones, again much less why one would want to work there or learn about business strategy or how to make sure the business flourished into the future," he wrote.

"Our real legacy was an inherited lack of awareness as to what it takes to nurture and pass on an effective legacy about what is really required to be responsible, engaged and active owners of a family business," Hill told family members.

If Hill's assessment is correct, a lack of family education was in large part responsible for the Bancroft family's loss of one of the most prestigious businesses in the world. The family had no teamwork, he concluded, and its members "never really figured out how to be owners."

Sooner or later, wise business-owning families see the necessity and desirability of launching some form of education for family members. Many of them make family-member education a central part of their mission. Consider, for example, the following excerpts of family mission statements from different families:

+ "To support each individual's efforts to develop [his or her] abilities..."
+ "...to allow each person to develop his or her maximum potential in ways that serve others."
+ "...to create an environment for lifelong learning..."
+ "...to enjoy learning about business, philanthropy, and life together..."

The intentions of this book are to explore the purposes and benefits of family education for enterprising families, to suggest possible topics for family education and development, to note the many vehicles available to families to support their efforts, and to raise some of the important issues involved in implementing an educational program.

What we have found in our many years of consulting and teaching is that family education is a very powerful tool that positions the family and its business for future success. Done well, a family education program offers many benefits: helping people prepare for their future roles and responsibilities in the business and in the family, providing a way of expressing care and commitment to each individual, earning loyalty from family members that reinforces their commitment to long-term ownership and stewardship, and strengthening the bonds among family members as they learn together and share life experiences and interests.

Our aim is to inspire you and your family to initiate a family education effort that is distinctly your own and is suited to the specific needs of your family. If your family is already engaged in education, this book will provide suggestions for enhancing your learning experiences. Very specifically, you will gain ideas for establishing a program, selecting courses that can be offered, finding the right instructors, and budgeting and paying for education. You will also learn about the factors that lead to success as well as the greatest challenges you are likely to face. And you will increase your understanding of when and why members of business-owning families need to come together for education and how education evolves over time. If you have already decided you need family education but you don't know where to begin, this book will get you started.

In many ways, family education is a team-building process. It will help the members of your family understand one another's strengths and weaknesses. It can create a more level playing field for family members and strengthen their voices in the family and its business. And it can—and, in our opinion, should—address the family as well as the business so that family members can be brought closer to one another not just to support the business, but also to reap the joy of healthier family relationships. In third and fourth generations (the "cousin" generations, when the family owners did not grow up together or in direct contact with the founding generation), we find that education can be the catalyst that enables family members to bridge old rifts and discover new friendships.

We have learned that the best education often comes from families sharing experiences with other families. Three chapters of this book and portions of other chapters provide you with knowledge that other families have gained in their own pursuit of education. What they have learned about conducting family education should be invaluable.

One family that discovered the power of education is the Lee family, owner of Lee Kum Kee Co. Ltd (LKK), a global producer of Chinese condiments and health products, founded in 1888 and based in Hong Kong. The four energetic Lee brothers in the fourth generation have overseen LKK's extraordinary expansion as they pursue a goal of reaching Chinese people around the world. By 2006, LKK had operations in China, Hong Kong, the United States, Malaysia, and the Philippines, and sold its products in 80 countries. But several years earlier, the brothers—Eddy, David, Charlie, and Sammy—and their sister Elizabeth began to worry about what would happen to the business when it became time to pass LKK to the next generation. The fifth generation consisted of 14 cousins ranging in age from two to 22, spread between the United States and Hong Kong. Most of those old enough to be thinking about careers expressed no interest in pursuing studies in the sciences or business, fields essential to LKK. For the most part, those cousins' knowledge of the business was informal and secondhand, often absorbed at family gatherings. They did not have the same emotional bond to the business that their parents had. And so engaged had the brothers been in building the business that they had not taken steps to address the next generation of leadership and ownership. They knew they had to act quickly, and they decided that family business education would be the key. Ultimately, their plan put family first, ahead of the business, as a way to enhance relationships and circumvent the rancor that the family had experienced in previous business successions.

As part of its education effort, the family began taking annual vacations together. Trips to Japan and Hawaii offered opportunities for learning about the business as well as having fun as a family. The Lee family council encouraged educational programs on the family's values, philosophies, and principles of management. To fill a communications gap, the fourth-generation mothers set up a "Super Mom Committee" to support contact among their kids and keep everyone informed about family and business news.

Other plans are in the making, and while it's too soon to tell what the ultimate results will be, the younger generation has responded positively. A 21-year-old budding artist has begun to think about how he might use his talent to contribute to the company, perhaps designing product labels. A 13-year-old said, "I didn't know too much about the family business until we started going on vacation together. But it's great to get the chance to know my cousins a little better."

EXHIBIT 1 **The Nine Benefits of Family Education**

1. Learning together brings extended family members closer to one another.
2. Cousins get to know and trust each other and learn how to work together as owners of the business and members of the family council.
3. The family business becomes stronger and healthier. The more educated family owners are, the easier it is for them to make better decisions about the business. They become assets to the business.
4. Family members who don't work in the business feel more connected to it. By taking responsibility for family education, they also have an opportunity to contribute to the enterprise and make an impact on it.
5. Cousins may put aside old family conflicts and discover they actually like each other.
6. Life becomes richer as family members enjoy new experiences together.
7. Family members reconnect with the community they grew up in when they return to plan or attend educational events.
8. Younger family members develop respect for employees by seeing how hard they work and how much they know.
9. Education instills pride in the family business and in the family and its values.

Chapter 2

The Evolution of Family Education

Family education evolves as businesses and their owning families grow and evolve. As family businesses go from being young and small to older and larger, the focus of education will shift. We generally find families progressing through these five phases.

PHASE 1: EDUCATION FOR FUTURE FAMILY EMPLOYEES AND MANAGERS

Business-founding parents very often first get interested in education once their children are teenagers and begin to be considered as prospective employees. The parents start to say, "We've got a 16-year-old and an 18-year-old. How do we introduce them to the business? How do we help them understand what their career choices are?" The parents begin to offer their children more background on the company and expose them to the business in ways that will help them make career decisions.

As the young people get involved in the company, perhaps as employees and managers, their education focuses on career development and preparation for higher levels of management. The family takes steps to make sure that the children's spouses understand what's going on in terms of the second generation from a managerial point of view.

PHASE 2: EDUCATION FOR SIBLING TEAM EFFECTIVENESS

It's often assumed that all the siblings in the second generation will join the business. As the second generation begins to contemplate joining the business, the family becomes more focused on education that will enhance the younger people's managerial skills in both the business and the family. The family concentrates on how its members work together as a team or as a group, and more emphasis is put on education to help increase the effectiveness of the family.

Families in this stage also focus on teaching interpersonal skills, such as communication proficiency and conflict resolution. The family initiates education about the business for the spouses so they have the understanding they need to support the enterprise.

PHASE 3: EDUCATION AS GOVERNORS AND OWNERS

As the family grows larger—perhaps entering the stage of cousin consortium—proportionately fewer family members work in the business. Nevertheless, some of those who do not join the business will become shareholders one day, while others will serve on the company's board of directors. Still others will play roles in the family business, serving on the family council, for example, or heading up a committee on philanthropy.

Now the family begins to raise new issues. Someone may say, "Clearly, some family members don't really understand the business as well as family members did in the past, when everybody worked in the business. And more people have roles as owners instead of as managers." Family members begin to ask, "What are the roles and responsibilities of owners? What are the owners' rights and privileges? What's the dividing line between being a manager and being an owner?"

On the governance side of things, family members begin to ask, "What do company boards do? How do they work? What's the relationship of the board to the company? To the owners? What kinds of people should we look for to be on the board?" Families may also start to raise similar questions about governance of the family itself: What is the role of a family council? How does a family council relate to the shareholder group and to the company board? What qualities should we be looking for in family leaders?

As a result of the new issues the family faces, it begins to concentrate on helping family members—particularly the cousins in the third generation—learn how to fulfill their roles as effective shareholders and competent governors of both the business and the family.

PHASE 4: EDUCATION FOR INHERITANCE

As wealth is transferred from one generation to the next, families seek ways to educate members about inheritance and affluence. Learning may focus on issues such as living with wealth, parenting children of privilege, security, philanthropy, public relations, and what it's like psychologically to bear both the blessings and burdens of wealth.

But inheritance is about more than just the transfer of money. Often, members of the third and fourth generation were born after the founding members passed away. Or family members are living far from where the family business is located, yet they feel a sense of identity or a pride of association with it. So education about inheritance also becomes education about inheritance of an identity; inheritance of a tradition, history, or legacy;

inheritance of reputation; and inheritance of responsibility, values, social contacts, and more.

PHASE 5: EDUCATION FOR LIFE

In this phase, the family asks, "Why should we educate just family members who are in management, who are going to be in governance or who are shareholders? Why don't we educate every family member so that everybody feels like an important part of our family, no matter what direction in life they choose?" When the family reaches this stage, it starts providing career development education for all family members who want it, not just for those headed for jobs in the family business. It looks for ways to involve the geographically distant family members in the life of the family, using education as a means. It takes on an attitude of "Let's support all family members in becoming successful and happy in whatever they do, in whatever role they play."

RECOGNIZING THE SIGNALS

You can have family education at any stage of a family business, but when you reach the third generation, the cousin consortium stage, it becomes imperative. It's inevitable that the larger, more diverse cousin group will become more removed from the business. The third-generation cousins are more diverse both geographically and in terms of lifestyles and interests. Unlike the second generation, when the siblings might have worked in the business, proportionately fewer cousins can do so. And that's when the family, in need of something to hold itself together and create the closeness and unity that will support the continuity of both family and business, wisely turns to education. Education becomes the key family glue. The family asks, "What kind of people are these cousins going to be? How do we prepare them to be owners someday? How do we provide education so that they enjoy each other, get to know each other and learn together?"

What other triggers alert the family to its need for education? Generational shifts are one. When the family sees the next generation coming up, it knows that the young people in it have to be readied in many ways. Even if the transition is from the much smaller first generation to the slightly larger second generation, the older family members recognize that their children need to learn about what's going on in the business or understand estate planning.

Still another trigger is that someone in the sibling generation, or perhaps the cousin consortium stage, says, "We really ought to do some planning together and make some decisions together." That kind of statement begins a phase of interpersonal learning aimed at helping family members work better as a team, communicate more effectively and make decisions as a group.

During the progression from one phase to another, families wake up to two realizations: First, over time, members have different education needs. And second, the family can make education available as a benefit for the entire family rather than as a resource only for those who are interested in the business.

EXHIBIT 2   The Five Phases of Family Education

1. Education for future employees and managers
2. Education for sibling team effectiveness
3. Education for governors and owners
4. Education for inheritance
5. Education for life

Chapter 3

Creating Your Curriculum

Who would have thought that teaching kids how to pick lemons could be a part of a family education curriculum? Well, the Leavens family, owners of the Leavens Ranches in Ventura and Monterey counties in California, did. Leavens Ranches is a thriving agricultural business that grows lemons, avocados, and grapes. The parents in the second generation and the nine cousins in the third generation all participate in the business in one way or another, but not all work in it. The Leavens family members are scattered across the United States and some live abroad. The family has grappled—successfully—with the issues of passing the business to the third generation, and the third generation has been taking its own long-range steps to ensure that the business passes on just as smoothly to the fourth generation and eventually to the fifth.

"The bigger issue for us is the challenge of having multigenerational owners," said David Schwabauer, a G3 (generation three) family member who works in the business. "You have to make sure there's a climate where the generations agree on a strategy to move the business forward before you go to an attorney to draw up documents."

There are 16 G3s in the company, now ranging from elementary-school age to mid-30s. Writing in the *FFI Practitioner*, Heather Leavens August, a G3 living in Firestone, Colorado, put it this way: "The G4s will need to be ready to take the reins and understand what the ranch is about, how important the family values are and what our history is, and also get to know each other so that they can work together when the time comes. And all this must happen without the benefit of having grown up on the ranch. None of this can happen by accident. It must be done deliberately."

Education is the key. At least once a year, the extended family members gather in Ventura for a week of fun and learning. There are business seminars and financial analysis for the adults, programs for the teenagers that help them understand their family business and how the ranches operate, and organized play for the younger children.

Then there's Camp Mary, a summer camp for the kids, named after the matriarch of the family, the eldest sibling in the second generation. Heather August describes it:

> In the summer of 2000, the first Camp Mary took place over three days. A committee met, including the parents of the participants as well as Mary, who is, by profession, an educator. We designed a curriculum that was specific to our family history, values, and industry, with activities and field trips. My brother gave the kids a lesson in lemon picking, which they did for two hours on the first day. This was not only to teach the logistics of the job, but also to make them appreciate how hard our employees work. In subsequent summers, they would work side-by-side with some of the most skilled workers in the business. My cousin David, who is the manager of the Fairview Ranch, our largest contiguous property, gave the kids a tour of the ranch, culminating with a stop at Aunt Mary's house for a swim and lessons in making "the perfect lemonade" and their own recipe for guacamole. Each day included a similar mix of learning and intergenerational fun.
>
> Over the years, Camp Mary has grown and changed with the children. It is now part of a company policy on youth employment, which includes Camp Mary (ages 5 through 12) as the starting section. The "13 through 16" Camp Mary covers more age-appropriate materials, includes more ranch work and lasts two weeks. Youth Employment begins at age 16. It runs for a period of up to four months during the summer. The last phase

is the first step toward a career with the company. This policy came out of the request from youth and their parents based on the philosophy that there should be an avenue for career development in the company ...

The process of designing a youth program model that works for our business has been difficult but rewarding work ... It is [based] on a belief in the future of the company, our grandparents' history, and ultimately our values and ethics, which provide the glue that holds the whole enchilada together.

Parents within the Leavens family take it upon themselves to encourage education that will support the business. One family member, a teenager from Bellevue, Washington, noted that her parents placed her in a Spanish immersion program at school. "I've been to Mexico, Honduras, and Costa Rica," she said. Being able to speak Spanish has helped her make friends on the ranch and also enabled her to have a better understanding of how things work in the business. "A lot of our farming activities are conducted in [Spanish]," she said.

FACTORS TO CONSIDER

How you design your family education program depends on many different factors:

- **The target audience.** Is it the family as a whole? A particular generation? Shareholders only? Spouses? Family members not working in the business?
- **The age of the audience you want to reach.** Young adults in their 20s or 30s? Teenagers? Young children?
- **The nature of your family business.** What industry are you in? What do family members need to know about the company specifically and the industry in general?
- **Your family's values.** Values will influence the topic choices you make. How much will you focus on the business? On philanthropy? On interpersonal relations and

getting to know one another? How much will you emphasize career development? Or governance? Or being good
shareholders?

What's important is that the topics you select meet your family's
specific needs. Later in this chapter, you will see what kinds of
topics four different families chose.

The impetus for family education can come from a variety
of sources. A group of family members can initiate it or just one
family member can champion it. Many times, financial and legal
advisors suggest it. Sometimes the push for it comes from very
smart non-family CEOs because they understand that a well-
educated ownership group is really an asset. CEOs, whether
or not they are family members, need the support of knowledgeable shareholders when big decisions are made. No matter
who initiates family education, however, the family needs to be
receptive and ultimately take responsibility and accountability
for it.

Who does the designing and chooses the courses? Ideally,
a small committee of family members takes responsibility for
developing and implementing family education. But these planners first find out what family members want and need to learn.
They seek ideas from all the family and take steps to get feedback from their "students" on the effectiveness of each educational event.

It's often wise to enlist professional help—not someone to
design the program for you, but someone who can offer ideas
and help your family achieve its education goals. The professional might be a family business consultant or an educator
experienced in working with family firms. The Leavens family
engaged two professionals: a family business consultant and a
university visiting professor with expertise in business leadership
and organizational change dynamics. When you bring in outside
assistance, you're not giving up control or ceding the responsibility of the design to someone else. Instead, you are looking to
your consultants to help you shape the program that meets your
family's needs most effectively.

WHAT TOPICS?

If you are just in the beginning stage of creating a family education program, you'll want to start slowly, choosing one or two topics initially and expanding as you go. As you gain more experience, your program can be more ambitious. Whatever stage you are in, however, there are many topics from which you can choose. We have found the following topics to be particularly important to business-owning families, and encourage you to seriously consider them as you develop your own curriculum. We've grouped these topics under four broad themes: family skills and understanding, career development, ownership knowledge, and governance preparation. You will see further on that we've suggested an alternative way of looking at these course ideas.

FAMILY EDUCATION TOPICS

I. Family Skills and Understanding

- **Interpersonal Skills.** How do family members work together to communicate, solve problems, address conflict, come to consensus, make decisions, and understand one another's different views?
- **Family History.** This includes the history of the family going back as far as you can, not just to when the patriarch or matriarch started the business. It also includes both sides of the family.
- **Family Dynamics.** This takes into account understanding how families work. For example, what are some of the classic communication problems within families? How do family members' different social styles or birth order affect things? What impact does the family tree have? Family dynamics focus more on how family relationships and family history impact current decision making and communications, whereas interpersonal skills concentrate on developing the ability to work together in a variety of ways.

- **Family Values.** What are the values that the family has articulated for itself? How have they changed over time? Grandparents can talk about the family's values to young grandchildren. Or, in a family meeting, members can talk about how the family's values have helped them make decisions or influenced their lives. A session might be centered on the question "Given our values, what kinds of conduct would we expect from the business?" (*Family Business Values: How to Assure a Legacy of Continuity and Success* is a good source of information on the topic.)

- **Personal Health.** Families often ask, "What kinds of things could we focus on together as a family that would be good for us as both individuals and a family?" As a result, a lot of families have sessions on health. Sometimes families will go to a spa or a clinic resort together. They might have a fitness or yoga instructor talk to them at a family meeting. If there's a family history of alcoholism, diabetes, heart disease, high blood pressure, high cholesterol, or other health problems that can be minimized through lifestyle changes, a family might bring in an expert to offer crucial insights. In short, family education can be used as a forum to encourage family members to adopt more informed health habits. Family meetings, we have found, can be the best and most intimate place to talk about issues that are specific to the family.

II. Career Development

- **Career Planning and Coaching.** Some families put as much emphasis on career development for those not interested in the business as for those who are. They reason that such education is important for all family members. In fact, helping and encouraging the next generation to find where its members really fit best is good for the business because it encourages those with the most aptitude for business to consider the family firm, while also encouraging those with other aptitudes to follow their hearts and talents in other pursuits. Education can help young people think about issues such as how people plan their careers, how to build networks, how to handle job interviews, and what makes for a good résumé. Education could also offer ideas on how to pursue a career and address questions such as "When should I get an advanced degree?" and "When does it make sense to change jobs?" Some families offer coaching to individual family members as a resource for their career planning, helping them to learn what their strengths, weaknesses, and aptitudes are.

- **Vocational Preferences.** While this is really a part of career planning, it is a subject that's useful to pull out as a separate topic. A career counselor can be brought in to help college or high school students understand the career directions that might be particularly suited to their strengths and interests. Tests can be administered to determine each individual's aptitudes.

- **Management Development.** This is more targeted to family members who are working in the business and are on an upward slope to becoming leaders in the company. Management development includes advice, counsel, and support, including things such as continuing education and university executive programs. It might also include 360-degree feedback, in which all the people around an individual (boss, peers, subordinates) offer their views on the person's strengths and weaknesses.

III. Ownership Knowledge

- **Business's History.** More than being just a recitation of dates and events ("In 1982, we appointed our first foreign distributor"), this topic should help family members understand the critical values of the business and its cultural and strategic evolutions. It should ask questions like: How did the changing business climate affect us? What made us abandon one business and get into another? What

opportunities did we see? What mistakes did we make?
What lessons did we learn?

+ **Financial Literacy Part I: Understanding Financial Statements.** This important topic is very popular among business-owning families. It includes subtopics such as how to read and interpret income statements and balance sheets. It also answers questions such as: What is return on invested capital? What is cash flow, where does it come from, and why is it important? In essence, the topic aims to help people understand the strategic plans for the business, to the extent that those plans are articulated through the numbers on the financial statements.

+ **Responsibilities and Roles of Ownership.** This topic is aimed at helping shareholders understand what they need to know so that they can support the company in the most effective way. It looks at issues such as what owners are responsible for, how they relate to the board of directors and to management, what owners should avoid (such as meddling), and what they can do (such as attend company cultural events) that's constructive.

+ **Estate Planning.** One of the topics of greatest interest to families, estate planning is also one of the trickiest. In some families, it brings up the question "Why are we discussing this? The person we're talking about isn't even dead yet." Often but not always taught by a lawyer, the topic explores issues such as what's currently in place in terms of estate planning; why estate planning is important; and how to understand estate plans, estate planning, and legal trusts. Family members might also share with one another what each has done in estate planning and what each has learned from the process.

+ **Financial Literacy Part II: Money and Investment Management.** While "Financial Literacy Part I" dealt with company finance, Part II deals with understanding how to manage and invest your personal money—that is, funds obtained outside the family firm or from dividends. Subtopics can include what to do with your 401(k) money, the power of compounding, and why saving and investing are good. Wealthier families might focus on how to invest, allocate assets, choose investment managers and understand the results of investing. To build interest among young people on the topic, you might create an investment club for them, letting them pick stocks and talk about how they made their choices. Younger family members can also be taught how to read the *Wall Street Journal* or how to calculate a price–earnings ratio or dividend yield. If yours is a large family that has personal money pooled together and looked after by a family office, your curriculum can include sessions on how to understand the office's reports about the family's assets. Younger family members also will need to learn how to think about the returns from their operating assets and how (whether even) to compare those to other possible investments.

- **Living with Wealth.** The key subtopic in this category is parenting children of privilege, and many sessions can be held on this subject alone. You can cover questions such as: What unique challenges do parents face when raising children with inherited wealth? Is wealth positive, negative, or neutral? What do you tell your children about the family's circumstances and when do you do it? How much do you tell them? How do you answer the questions your children ask? How do you prepare them for the ways in which people in their schools or their communities relate to them and treat them? How do you answer the insensitive (but possibly innocent) questions that people ask you or your children? How do you manage differences that may exist between you as a couple in this area?

    Coping with inherited wealth is a common and important topic. Families find that this subject in particular lends itself to within-the-family sharing. No one else can really understand the issues that come from the family's history, name, and financial circumstances.

    The broad topic "living with wealth" can also address the matter of procuring physical security for the family or managing relationships with in-laws' families when they have lesser means.

- **Philanthropy.** Issues covered can include the family's philanthropic history and what the company is giving in the way of charitable contributions or the philanthropic initiatives it has established. Together, family members can explore theories of philanthropy, looking at issues such as what motivates giving, how to create helpful guiding principles for giving, how to provide oversight, and how to evaluate proposals—in other words, how to practice philanthropy most effectively. In some families, the members focus on learning about how and why to do philanthropy jointly. In families where charitable contributions are made separately, family members may come together to share their experiences and learn from one another. The Schmidt family of U.S. Oil Co., Inc., discussed in Chapter 6, offers an excellent example of a family engaged in learning about philanthropy.

- **Understanding Foundations and Family Offices.** Some larger successful families establish family foundations to handle their giving and family offices to manage investments or perform administrative and other services for the extended family. Families need to know how to govern the institutions they have created, understanding how they work and what their structures are. Classes can be built around questions such as: How do foundations work? How are funding decisions made and who makes them? How are grants monitored? How do family offices function and how do they pay for themselves? How do you govern a family office? What makes for an effective family office? What services are available from ours and why aren't others offered? What's the cost? How is information about these two institutions—the foundation and the family office—communicated to the family?

PREPARATION FOR GOVERNANCE

- **Understanding Boards and Business Governance.** Younger family members, the 20-somethings, generally don't know what a board of directors is and what it does. They don't understand what kinds of decisions boards make, how they function, and the rules and bylaws under which they must operate. A session or two can be developed to help young people—and older family members too—understand these and other issues. The "students" can begin to learn what a good board looks like and how a board's performance is evaluated. They can learn what committees a board has, what the function of each is, and how a committee relates to the board as a whole.

- **Preparation for Board Service.** The foregoing course is a prerequisite to this one, which covers how a family member can prepare to be a good board member, what the qualifications are, and what to look for when selecting a board candidate. As a teaching tool, some families create "shadow" board meetings at which family members play the roles of board members, going through a real agenda, having discussions, and making decisions just as a real board does. This exercise helps people get an idea of how the board thinks and the decisions it makes.

Some families create forums at which family members interact with the company's independent directors, asking questions such as: What does the board do and how does it work? If I were interested in being on the board, what kinds of background skills and knowledge must I have and what courses might I take? What kind of experience do I need? Still other families invite a limited number of family members to observe board meetings as part of their educational process. A family member who wants to gain broader knowledge might also observe board committee meetings or even be invited to sit on a committee. These special educational roles are often called "board observers" or even "junior board members."

Caution: Make it clear to family members that taking the board preparation class does not guarantee them a seat on the board. It is only a beginning step, but one that will help them better understand the process.

♦ **Understanding Business Strategy and Culture.** To be good governors—not necessarily good board members, but good owners—requires at least a broad grasp of the company's strategy so that each person understands what the company is doing, the decisions that are being made, and the risks that the company is taking. How does our company compare to other companies in our industry? What pressures and opportunities are facing our industry right now? It is important to understand the strategy in the context of the industry and market—and even international and national forces—in your particular sector of the economy. Education helps family members understand what is meant by the word "strategy," what the elements of a strategy are, and how the strategy aligns with the family's goals and values, which are often achieved through a parallel planning process. The same goes for company culture. Families usually want their members to be supportive of the values of the company and its culture, or at least to know that the culture appropriately fits with the family values. Even if they don't work in the company, they may visit the company or attend company ceremonies. Education sessions can help family members understand what "company culture" means, what its ingredients are and how to pass on a good company culture. They can learn how employees are trained in terms of culture and what they are told in the employee newsletters and orientation programs about the family's culture and values. Responsible owners need to know enough about strategy to support it and need to understand enough about culture to contribute to it. In fact, the family's values often shape the corporate culture, so it's good to understand how that takes place.

♦ **Understanding Family Councils and Family Governance.** These are counterparts to business boards and business, since family councils are the governance body for the family. The topic covers issues such as what a family council and its mandate are; what decisions it makes; its composition, officers, committees, roles, and terms of service; how the election process works; the rules under which it operates; how it interfaces with the board and management; and what the family's expectations of the council members should be. Education on these issues should provide an understanding of what family councils do for the family business and the family itself.

- **Understanding the Family's Constitution.** A family constitution or protocol consists of all the agreements a family has made to perpetuate the family and its business. It includes the shareholder's agreement (e.g., buy–sell agreement, redemption process); the formal policies that govern family interaction with the business (e.g., employment rules or the process for evaluating family employees); and a statement of the family philosophy, including its values and mission.

  Education will help family members understand what a constitution is, why having one is important, what it comprises, and what makes a good constitution. Family members will also learn how their constitution is specific to their family, what the history of its development is, how decisions are made, and even the process for making changes to it.

- **Family Leadership and Facilitation Skills.** The family needs members who will step up to be the leaders of the family council and skillful facilitators of family meetings, as well as leaders of specific committees. Through courses, seminars, or off-site family business conferences, family members can learn more about the leadership opportunities available in the family and how to prepare themselves for these important roles.

EXHIBIT 3 **Top Six Family Education Topics**

Based on the authors' experience, here are the education topics of greatest interest to business-owning families:

1. Communications and conflict management skills
2. Parenting children of privilege and wealth
3. Estate planning
4. Financial literacy

5. Business literacy
6. Group and family dynamics

MIX, MATCH, REPACKAGE

Obviously, many of the topics we've suggested can't be handled in a one-hour session. They have many subtopics and often lend themselves to multiday seminars and workshops. You can mix, match, and repackage topics. For example, you can put philanthropy together with foundations, leaving family offices separate. Families without foundations or family offices will leave those topics out but still want to address philanthropy.

You may also want to consider renaming or reorganizing the broad categories of topics we have suggested. Some families might find it more useful to organize their curriculum in the way shown below in Exhibit 4.

EXHIBIT 4 **Our Family Education Curriculum**

A. **Understanding Families and Individuals**
  1. **Understanding Our Family and Ourselves**
     a. Our Family History
     b. Our Family Values
     c. Our Family Philanthropy
     d. Our Individual and Group Communication Styles
     e.
     f.
  2. **Business-Owning Families and Individuals**
     a. Raising Children of Privilege/Wealth Psychology
     b. Trends in Philanthropy
     c. Security and Risk Management
     d.
     e.

3. Interpersonal Skills/Family Systems
   a. Healthy Family Dynamics and Family Systems
   b. Understanding Adult Development and Parent–Child/Adult–Child Relationships
   c. Listening and Communication Styles
   d. Conflict Management/Decision Making/Problem Solving
   e. Team Building
   f. Leading and Managing Meetings and Projects
   g. Presentation Skills
   h.
   i.

B. Understanding Our Business, Family Business, and Business in General
   1. Our Business
      a. Its History
      b. Its Values and Culture
      c. Company Strategy and Governance Structure
      d. Industry Insights: Suppliers, Customers, Competitors, Trends, and Challenges
      e. Our Marketing and Branding
      f. Interesting Issues (e.g., workplace diversity, consumer health, global culture, ethical problems, media and public relations, innovations, environment/sustainability, business partnerships)
      g. Company Philanthropy and Community Involvement
      h.
      i.
   2. Family Business
      a. Family Business 101
      b. Roles and Responsibilities of Owners
      c. Preparing for Family Leadership Roles
      d. Estate Planning
      e. Knowing Our Advisors/Trustees

> f. Family Governance
> g. Our Family Constitution, Code, and Policies
> 3. **General Business**
>   a. Understanding Financial Statements
>   b. Business Boards
>   c. Business Strategy
>   d. Law for Business Owners
>   e. Management's Needs and Perspectives
>   f. The World of Economics
>   g.
>   h.

Exhibit 4 may serve as a helpful checklist or survey around which to design an educational curriculum.

VEHICLES THAT SUPPORT EDUCATION

Probably the most common form of education is a workshop conducted by a consulting resource person, advisor, or invited expert during a family meeting. But we have also seen families successfully utilize a variety of other vehicles and venues:

- Internships in the family's business or in another family-owned company
- Family newsletter articles
- Family business websites
- The family's own private website for family members
- Professional association memberships and courses
- Family business executive education courses at universities
- Participation in family business centers and forums
- Attendance at seminars offered by banks, family business consulting firms, family business centers associated with colleges and universities, the Family Business Network, and other institutions
- Investment clubs

- Career or personal development camps or courses
- Field visits
- Job exchanges with other families in business or philanthropy
- Junior boards of directors
- Family foundation boards or nonprofit boards
- Observing at company board meetings or family councils
- Personal mentors in and/or out of the business
- Developmental coaches
- Family council projects or task forces
- Service on boards of other organizations
- Retreats for next-generation team building
- Memberships in the Young Presidents Organization, TEK groups, or other leadership peer groups
- Networking with management and independent directors of the family's business

There are no limits to the possibilities. We find that families mix and match the vehicles for different topics, using one vehicle—the family website, for example—to reinforce the learning gained in another, such as a family meeting.

The Taylor/Bitzer family, which owns ABARTA, Inc., in Pittsburgh, came up with a particularly creative vehicle. ABARTA owns soft-drink bottling companies, newspapers, and some real estate development and oil and gas companies. In 2001, the third generation launched "Future Shareholders' Days," held about every 18 months, to educate the 17 members of the fourth generation, then ages eight to 20 years, about the business. One Future Shareholders' Day involved a trip to ABARTA's newspaper in Atlantic City, New Jersey, where the children toured the plant and watched the printing of a special edition that featured them. On another Shareholders' Day, the children visited a cave to learn about oil and gas drilling.

FAMILY THEMES

Depending on the variables we mentioned earlier in this chapter, family education programs tend to evolve around certain themes. Developing interpersonal skills is critical for smaller families because these skills make consensus-building and conflict management less challenging. Larger multigenerational families with well-established businesses are typically more interested in philanthropy, public service, a family office, or active direct investments. Here are brief examples of how four families with very different needs chose to approach family learning.

Family #1: Focus on Business Dynamics

A multibillion-euro Scandinavian firm with about 200 family shareholders created an education committee that included the CEO, board chairman, family council chairman, and an outside consultant. The committee decided to focus on the dynamics of running a successful family business, so they conducted three two-day workshops each year covering the following topics:

- How family businesses work
- The global role of family firms
- The family firm's business strategy
- Accounting and finance
- The challenges of succession and continuity
- The family's values and the business's culture
- The roles and responsibilities of the board
- The history and function of the family council

Family #2: Exploring Shared Personal Interests

A large family with shared interests in passive investments and philanthropy as well as limited involvement in its operating companies elected a family committee to devise an annual four-day reunion. Designed to develop strong ties within the extended family and help family members pursue shared personal interests, the program included:

- A family question-and-answer session after the annual shareholder meeting
- A young children's program for play, fun, and adventure

- A family Olympics of silly games that has become a tradition
- Workshops on college and career planning featuring panels of older family members
- Distinguished speakers to stimulate a fresh view of world events
- A presentation by another large business-owning family
- A series of six elective workshops that include the areas of personal development, family values, and understanding business and philanthropy

Family #3: Developing the Next Generation

A family with ten young-adult and teenage cousin shareholders-to-be who will inherit a trust with substantial ownership responsibilities of a large diversified company hired a full-time family education mentor to oversee a multiyear program that includes:

- A one-week course, "Finance for Nonfinancial Managers"
- Four-week assignments in family office, family foundation, and family history
- Working one summer as an hourly employee in one of the family's manufacturing plants
- A two-month assignment in three of the following areas: corporate finance, manufacturing, sales and marketing, information services, research and development, and corporate development
- Two years of outside work experience in a related industry
- An internship in a corporate or investment banking firm
- Mini-courses in personal financial management, time management, family business, and philanthropy
- Completion of a research paper on a family business topic that requires visits to several other family firms

Family #4: Building Strong Family Ties

A family business with 7 third-generation adult members and 15 fourth-generation children under the age of 12 used a facilitator to plan workshops at two weekend family meetings per year. This family's education focus is on:

- Parenting
- Coping with inherited wealth
- Listening skills, including videotaped role-playing
- Personal styles, including sharing results of the Myers-Briggs Type Indicator, a personality questionnaire
- Confrontation and conflict management

While their parents are in the workshops, younger children usually attend a sports and activities camp that emphasizes team-building and leadership. The family regularly invites business owners from other families to discuss their own family relationship-building experiences.

Part II of this book, "Meeting Your Family's Particular Needs," offers an in-depth look at how three different families went about creating three very individual education efforts.

Chapter 4

Getting Down to Logistics

There's more to family education than curriculum. Just as journalists have to include the who, what, when, where, why, and how in their stories, planners have to include additional specific elements in their education programs to make the effort succeed. The "what" is primarily the curriculum, which we discussed at length in Chapter 3. The additional elements about which we receive questions most often are:

- How often?
- Who attends?
- Who teaches?
- Who is "dean"?
- Who pays?
- What venues?
- What expectations?

Let's take these one by one.

HOW OFTEN?

We generally advise families to have at least two family meetings a year and to devote a substantial portion of each meeting to education. There are many ways to approach this. One is to devote about one-quarter of each meeting to education. The other three-quarters would go equally to policy/decision making, providing updates, and having social fun. If a family can plan educational meetings four to six times a year, so much the better. For many families, however, such frequency may not be feasible. Still, other families are so convinced of the importance of education that they plan educational meetings even more often. Many families find ways to weave education into other activities and publications, such as internships, newsletters, e-mails, and family websites.

EXHIBIT 5   The Four Elements of a Family Meeting

1. Education
2. Providing information/updates
3. Policy/decision making
4. Having fun

The stories of different families in this book offer a variety of ways to answer "How often?" You have seen, for example, how the Leavens family concentrated on its youth-education program in the summer, when most members of the target audience were available.

It's important to build momentum and encourage participation by having regularly scheduled sessions planned far in advance. Get into some kind of rhythm so that you don't suddenly realize it has been two or three years since you had an educational get-together.

It also helps to look for windows of opportunity. We find that families go through periods when people are heavily engaged in family participation and other periods when they appear more disconnected. Capitalize on those periods of more intense involvement. An example might be when members of the next generation are in their early 20s, perhaps just coming out of college. They are often not yet burdened by family ties and the obligations of homes, jobs, and kids, so it's an ideal time to get them interested in family enterprise education.

WHO ATTENDS?

In our view, the answer to "Who attends?" is "everybody," but not necessarily all at the same time. Deciding on who attends will depend on the attendees' age, position in the family (direct descendant or in-law), whether they are shareholders, the family's culture, and so on. We've known families that welcome everybody, including in-laws, because they think the open sharing of knowledge and information is the best policy. They also believe that including everyone builds a stronger family team.

We've known families that provide education only to those who are owners of or employed in the business. We've also known families that prefer to provide education to direct descendants only, therefore excluding in-laws. In cultures still wedded to the notion that ownership must be limited to the males in the family, this might mean excluding the women. Although we do not customarily encourage these more exclusive approaches, we do recommend that family culture and tradition play important roles in how inclusion decisions are made.

Those families that favor offering education for everyone often reason that learning about the family and its business helps everyone understand and support the family firm. So they include not only shareholders and family members working in the business, but also those who don't own shares, those who don't work in the business, and the spouses of all family members. They recognize that non-owners or non-employees might also include future owners or future managers.

Age is an important factor in determining who attends. You need to gauge what young people are ready to learn. Preschoolers obviously are not going to sit through a discussion on how to read a balance sheet. But creative families have conducted programs geared for children as young as six years old, and some families have found that intergenerational programs that are fun for all have important benefits. Learning together can create lasting bonds between parents and kids that strengthen both family and business and help support the passing of the business safely to the next generation. Just remember to emphasize the fun.

Intergenerational programs don't work when they consist of the "old" lecturing younger family members and telling them what to do and think. Even when multigenerational programs are taught by a skilled trainer, it's a good idea to have breakout sessions of peer groups so that young people can interact with one another out from under the eyes of parents or grandparents.

If you have two family meetings a year, the educational sessions at one meeting might be inclusive of all family members, while at the second meeting the education might be divided into segments, with topics designed to match appropriate audiences.

Should you include key non-family executives or non-family shareholders as students in your family education sessions? We think not. Although the instructors may be non-family, the audience needs to be family members. Family education is meant to be an intimate learning experience, one that encourages family sharing and team building. The presence of outsiders interferes with both the sharing and the team building.

WHO TEACHES?

For those programs you conduct "in house," you'll need to identify and secure good teachers. We find that you can uncover excellent instructors in a lot of different nooks and crannies. The choice of teacher depends on both the subject matter and the audience. Here are some possibilities:

- ◆ Local colleges and universities are often good places to find resource people who teach courses on interpersonal skills, personal development, and some of the business topics.
- ◆ Executive directors or leaders of trade associations can be interesting because they can talk about your industry in the broadest terms and offer the "big picture."
- ◆ Some families bring in resource people who are experts in their fields to provide a special experience and inspire the family. For example, sports figures, coaches, and people who have overcome adversity make good speakers.

- Your family's professional advisors—accountants or lawyers, for example—can be called in if they have good teaching skills. A lawyer can help family members understand trusts or how boards work, while an accountant can provide instruction on estate planning or business.
- Many families turn to their own businesses for expert help. Young people enjoy learning from employees what their jobs are all about. A company human resources manager might be a skilled trainer in the area of career development. The financial staff might be called on to put together some sessions on finance. One wealthy family we know brought in the company's security chief to talk to family members about how to protect themselves and be safe while traveling.

  Look to other family businesses. Many families find value in bringing representatives of other families to their family meetings to talk about specific topics and share their experiences.
- Family members themselves can serve as instructors or facilitators under certain circumstances. One of the best uses of family members occurs when some go off specifically to gain knowledge and then bring back what they've learned to share with the rest of the family. A group of family members might visit other countries where the family does business and, upon their return, make a presentation to the rest of the family on what they learned. Individuals who attend family business conferences or seminars at home or abroad can bring back information to share at family meetings or in a family newsletter.

  Family members can also take turns and lead educational sessions, as long as the rest of the family understands that these instructors are volunteers, not professional trainers, and that they are doing it for their own personal development. In such cases, family members turn out to offer their support. And that's a good thing.

  Do exercise caution about involving family members as instructors, however. Even if a family member has expert knowledge on a topic, it's usually wiser to bring in an outside resource person to do the teaching. An exception might be if the family is really comfortable with the family member and extends an invitation for him or her to teach. (At times, when an in-law or family member not working in the business has an expertise that people truly want to tap, it can help to bring that person into the fold.) Otherwise, keep in mind that educational sessions are not meant to be occasions for one family member to show off his or her knowledge. The goal is to create an atmosphere were everybody feels comfortable. Family members might feel embarrassed or hesitant to show what they don't know if a family member is the teacher. And whoever does teach should start at a very basic level. You might be surprised at how many people who ostensibly know a lot about business can still really benefit from starting with the basics. Fundamentals are always valuable, so starting at the beginning helps set a level playing field.

Where do you begin to look for instructors? Ask your local college, trade association, and professional advisors whom they might suggest. Other family businesses are also good sources of referrals. (See "Resources" on page 85.)

WHO'S THE "DEAN"?

"Who's 'dean'?" simply means "Who's leading the charge of our family education program?" The dean is basically the one who champions, organizes, and guides the process. It could be an individual in the family who volunteers and says, "Yes, I'll take responsibility for this." It could be a committee appointed by the family council. In some cases, families ask a family business consultant to take on this role in addition to that person's more typical consulting activities. Sometimes a family will hire, on a consulting basis, someone from a local college who is expert at adult development and adult education. Such a consultant will be charged with taking leadership of the education effort, making recommendations to the family about what education it needs and finding the right people to do the teaching. Sometimes the responsibility rotates to keep it more manageable and bring different styles and perspectives to the task.

If it's a larger, sophisticated, more complex family, the family office might be used to guide and administer the education program. The responsibility might be part of the job of a staff member or even a full-time employee whose position focuses solely on family education. One such dean shares her experience and insights in Chapter 7.

In addition to advising the family on its educational needs and securing instructors, deans help families decide whether certain topics need to be repeated so that family members can build skills, recommend venues for learning events, determine if there should be homework, and research and recommend outside courses that family members can attend.

WHO PAYS?

Budgeting for family education is a sign that the family takes education seriously. It means that it's formalizing education by designating a sum of money and saying, "We are committed to ongoing family education and willing to establish a budget for that purpose. We're willing to invest in education, be accountable and responsible for deploying these funds, and stay fully conscious of all costs." What's more, budgeting for education is a good discipline that also fosters fairness. You want to establish policies and processes that ensure fair access to educational resources.

We estimate that 80 to 90 percent of the families involved in family business education have their business pay for it. The cost is usually funded by "shareholder relations." Families that do this say, "This is a very important and legitimate business expense. We're training and developing our shareholders and our shareholders-to-be, equipping them to be responsible and capable contributors." Many times, family councils are granted budgets that are funded by the company, and "education" appears as a line item in the family council budget.

Other families feel that it's more appropriate for the family to pay. Some project the cost of education on a periodic (often annual) basis, divide it up and charge it back to individual family members. Or when the family council is funded by the family (sometimes through assessments or dues), education is a part of the council's budget. In some instances, the family office pays for it. In others, the senior generation pays for education as a gift to the whole family. Sometimes there is stock granted to the family office or family council (from a trust), and it funds education and other family related expenses. What should your education budget include? Give some thought to these possible costs: travel expenses for attendees and resources; fees for outside speakers; the cost of hiring a consultant to help you plan your education program or run it if family members don't; group meals of attendees; facility-related expenses such as meeting rooms, if they must be rented; rental fees for audiovisual or teleconferencing equipment and services; and office supplies and materials. And how about paying for fun, memorable team-building events that keep the education fresh and participative? Some families even pay the personal expenses of family members for child support sessions. Other families pay members for the time they spend planning and organizing educational sessions.

The size of your budget will depend on factors such as how many family members you have and how widely scattered they are. Families with sons and daughters overseas may decide that they will pay to bring the kids back once a year or once every two years, but not four times a year. Smaller families or those whose members still live close to home can get by with a more modest allowance for travel.

There is another cost that won't appear in your budget but that needs to be considered because it is the most precious and dear resource there is: time. There might be homework or preparation that will require time from the family members in addition to the time they will spend in attendance. There will certainly be time expended by family volunteers who plan your program or by family members who serve as instructors. If you ask family or non-family executives in your business to speak at some sessions, they are taking time from your business or their families to meet your request. It's important to be aware of the cost of time and to respect it as you move forward with your program. Also—another time-related dilemma—when should you meet? For those working in the business, meeting during the workweek can be fairly easy. For those with jobs or commitments outside the family business, they may have to take vacation time or personal days in order to participate in education. This latter group may prefer to meet on the weekend, while those who work in the business may prefer to meet during the workweek. Additionally, including parents in educational sessions requires that attention be paid to child-care considerations. Many families choose to pay for child care or make arrangements that facilitate the participation of parents in these sessions.

WHAT VENUES?

Where should your educational sessions be held? Almost any venue will work, as long as it's appropriate. Small sessions can be conducted in meeting rooms or conference rooms at the business. Large groups might require renting space at a hotel or conference center. Just make sure that the room arrangements support the learning experience. Can everyone see and hear? Would tables in a U shape work better than seats facing a podium?

And be imaginative. A visit to one of your company's facilities or to another family-owned business can be both fun and informative. And as the Leavens ranching family discovered, a lemon orchard is the perfect spot for some learning. Informal settings can offer great environments for education. As many business-owning families recognize, some of the greatest learning among the young takes place day after day at the dinner table.

Rotate among simple, local, low-cost, short, straightforward events and more extensive, expensive, memorable, educational experiences. You may want to plan a real blowout event every three years or so. Schedule the event a year in advance to promote attendance. Getting an event planned and organized in such a way that folks can attend is truly one of the biggest challenges. And at the same time, you must be realistic and know that everyone won't be able to come to every event. Switching things up in terms of location, timing, length, and format rather than doing the same thing over and over will increase the chance that a variety of folks will attend. Be careful that things aren't planned and organized by the same people year after year, which might lead to exclusion of others.

WHAT EXPECTATIONS?

Education planners need to be sure that they are not misleading family members and raising false expectations. There needs to be clarity about the fact that even though certain information is shared with them, family members won't necessarily play a specific role in the future. For example, as mentioned earlier, family members need to know that participating in a session on how boards work in a family business does not necessarily mean they will sit on the board someday. Attending a meeting on how a given department works or on the business's strategy should not be taken as signals that a family member even should work in the business. Make it clear why a given topic has been selected so that family members can adjust their expectations accordingly: "This knowledge will help me be a better shareholder," for example, or "This class can help me understand career development, whether or not I work in the business. If I aspire to join the business, I'll have a better understanding of where I can fit in and I'll know what qualifications I have to meet."

The students in your family will have expectations that the education program will need to meet. They want to know that if they take the time to show up at sessions, the instructors will be well prepared and the materials well crafted. They also have a right to expect an appropriate learning environment.

The program planners and instructors will have some expectations of their students, too, in terms of comportment and dress. Some planners have been embarrassed when they have lined up an important speaker only to have the college-age attendees come dressed as they would for a very casual university class. Or there's frustration when cousin Rebecca flies in from Alaska for a meeting, but cousin Paul won't even drive down the street for the same event or cousin Hannah ditches because she has the sniffles.

What program planners need to do to avoid such situations is prepare family members. Let them know if they are expected to dress professionally, and establish a code of conduct. That will be part of their learning process, too. Balancing informality and tolerance with professionalism is always an art for families. Also, the more involved people are, the greater the opportunity they have to influence the shape of the sessions and topics covered, and the more likely it is that they will be present and will participate appropriately.

PART II

MEETING YOUR FAMILY'S PARTICULAR NEEDS

When it comes to family education programs, no one size fits all. You can't just take the topics we suggested in Chapter 3 and say, "Great. Here's a ready-made curriculum we can use." Some topics will be appropriate for your family, but others will not. You will want to pick and choose from our suggestions and probably add ideas that we haven't mentioned. The beauty of custom-designing your own program is that you can create a course of study that suits the unique needs of your family and its individual members.

Consider the families in the next three chapters and think about how they are alike, how they are different, and what distinguishes the approach to family education in each.

Chapter 5

The Rodales

A Fourth-Generation Initiative

Even if you don't know who the Rodales are, you probably are familiar with some of their company's products. Based in Emmaus, Pennsylvania, and New York City, Rodale, Inc., publishes magazines such as *Men's Health, Organic Gardening, Prevention,* and *Runner's World.* Its book division is known for bestsellers such as *The South Beach Diet* series and Al Gore's *An Inconvenient Truth.*

A visionary who believed that people could achieve better health by cultivating healthier soil using natural techniques, J. I. Rodale founded a small publishing company in 1930. He started *Organic Farming and Gardening* magazine in 1942 and introduced *Prevention* in 1950. Now international in scope, Rodale, Inc., spreads the message of health and wellness through its publications in more than 40 countries, including South Africa, Russia, Greece, China, the United Kingdom, France, and Germany. The company, which has an online presence, employs more than 1,000 people.

Several years ago, two members of the fourth generation (G4)—Maya Rodale and Shelbi R. Gourniak—began to realize they needed to know more about the company. By virtue of family trusts, they and all nine of their siblings and cousins were shareholders in the company. Whether or not the G4 family members worked in the company, Maya and Shelbi knew they all needed a better understanding of Rodale, Inc., in order to be effective owners.

The G4 cousins ranged from one toddler to one 30-year-old, with most concentrated in their 20s. All the older G4s wanted to know more about the family business, according to Shelbi, "but Maya and I actively stepped up and said, 'We are extremely interested. We want to be educated. We want to know what we're doing internally so that when people ask us questions, we know what's going on.'"

Fueled by their interest, Maya, a romance novelist, and Shelbi, an MBA who joined the family company in an Advertising Operations role in March 2008, took on the leadership of the G4 Education Program—or what they call "G4 EDU." They work as partners, with Maya planning some sessions and Shelbi overseeing others.

The earliest topics, says Maya, were "obvious choices." They brought in the family lawyer to explain the family trusts, which Maya describes as "tricky and complicated, and we all say you need to hear about them 20 times before you understand them. I'm not there yet."

They followed with presentations by some of Rodale's employees—the editor-in-chief of *Men's Health*, a magazine design director and a book cover artist, for example. Employees have also conducted sessions on new-product development, book production, and Rodale's custom publishing group, which publishes newsletters and magazines for other companies. Later, the family business consultant led sessions on how ownership and cousin groups work together and on communication styles and cousin teamwork. On the whole, Rodale's program focuses on educating G4s about what their business does. Shelbi and Maya have surveyed their cousins on how they feel about the program content and logistics and have asked for topic ideas. They found that the group wanted to know more about the company's online businesses, marketing, magazine circulation, production, printing, photography and imaging, and budgeting and finance. They also wanted to learn about philanthropy and the Rodale Institute, a nonprofit research farm near Kutztown,

Pennsylvania. They showed interest in learning about teamwork and getting a greater understanding of publishing as an industry. One cousin, Marlow Rodale, an aspiring artist, made a pitch for a trust-building workshop for the cousins. "We are going to have to work together even if we're not all working within the company," he observes. By the way, this is very common—next-generation folks are customarily bored by the "softer" topics and most compelled by specifics, tangible information, exposure to the products, and people that make up their businesses.

G4 EDU has one rule: no parents allowed. Only members of the fourth generation are permitted at these learning events. "Part of what we wanted to achieve was bonding as a group and getting to know each other in this setting and capacity, as opposed to childhood memories like playing in the dirt," explains Maya. Besides, the parents already knew much of what the cousins wanted to learn, and, says Maya, "we wanted the program to definitely focus on us." She also notes that it means a lot to the cousins that the parents let them be "unchaperoned" in this undertaking.

"We want to really keep it more informal and more educational, versus having a parent or aunts or uncles sitting in there and changing the mood of the session," adds Shelbi. She and Maya were aiming for an atmosphere in which the cousins could feel totally free to ask questions about the company. Fourth-generation spouses are welcome. Even though the third generation is not invited to the G4 EDU programs, the fourth generation keeps the whole family informed. Maya initiated a family newsletter called "The Loop" that includes a write-up on each G4 session. The newsletter offers any G4 cousin who couldn't attend a meeting a way to catch up and also keeps the parent generation apprised of what's going on at the G4 events. She assigns someone else to do the write-up, which not only relieves her of writing it herself, but also assures active participation by other cousins. Also, Maya and Shelbi are officers on the Rodale Family Council, a forum they use as an additional means of communication with their family about the G4 program.

G4 EDU isn't the only vehicle of education in the Rodale family. Learning also takes place at biannual all-family meetings. One time, Peter Post of the Emily Post Institute was brought in to lead a session on business etiquette that Maya recalls as "really fantastic."

The Rodales also have a family business conference policy under which family members can apply for funds to attend seminars and conferences offered by a list of preapproved organizations such as the Family Business Network (FBN) in Lausanne, Switzerland; Loedstar in Geneva, Switzerland; and INSEAD in Fontainebleau, France. (See "Resources," p. 85.) "So you just apply, you go, you enjoy it, you learn stuff, and then you write about it for 'The Loop,'" says Maya, who recently attended a Loedstar conference in London. Shelbi once went with her sister, Sarah Stoneback, and their aunt, Heidi Rodale, to Cannes, France, to attend an FBN seminar. "It was really incredible to meet siblings and cousins from other countries and other family businesses and understand how they interact with each other and how they're learning in their own businesses," says Shelbi. In an effort to learn more about their company's industry, some of the G4s also have attended the Magazine Publishers of America "Magazine University," a five-week, once-a-year lecture series.

Young family members can also participate in a Rodale internship program, but they're not guaranteed a spot just because they are family members. To avoid nepotism or its perception, Marlow says, family members "have to go through the same process that everyone else has to go through in order to apply for and actually get accepted to these internships."

RODALE FAMILY EDUCATION LOGISTICS

Each learning session lasts about two hours and takes place in Rodale offices in either Emmaus or New York City. Initially, Maya and Shelbi expected to hold sessions once a month, but reality set in. With so many of the G4s still in college and people somewhat geographically scattered, such frequency was not possible. Now the planners aim for four meetings a year, clustering them during winter breaks or the summer. Meeting less frequently wards off the resentment that can build when people feel too heavy an infringement on their time.

Average attendance is four or five of the eight adult cousins. Of the three youngest cousins, a 14-year-old attends sessions when she is able.

G4 and other family education costs are paid out of the company budget for owner expenses. Covered are expenses such as travel, meals, approved conferences, and speakers. (Employees who make presentations, however, do not receive extra remuneration.) They consulted the company expense reimbursement policy and established their own.

THE ROLE OF VALUES

A family's values, either consciously or unconsciously, will have an influence on the design of any family education effort and how it's carried out. "The number one thing we strive for is transparency, and every effort is made to keep everyone informed," says Maya about the Rodale G4 EDU program. When she says "everyone," she means the third generation, too, even though its members aren't invited to the sessions. When an e-mail is sent out to the G4 members letting them know the particulars of the next meeting, the G3s are copied "just so they know," says Maya. "And we write that article [about the meeting] in the family newsletter that everyone sees."

The values she cites are inclusion and respect. Everyone eligible is invited to the meetings, but if someone can't attend or doesn't want to, Maya says, "that's fine. But you're always going to be invited, and every effort is going to be made to accommodate you." There's no insistence, however, and no laying guilt on people if they can't attend.

The family's and the company's overarching values—taking care of one's personal health and protecting the environment—are played out in subtle ways. Marlow recalls learning more about the history of the company and the mission of his great-grandfather, J. I. Rodale, in one of the G4 sessions. And as a result of attending presentations by company employees, he grew increasingly aware and proud that talented people left very prestigious companies to come to Rodale because they liked its work environment and believed in the company's message.

BENEFITS: EXPECTED AND UNEXPECTED

One of the most important and most unexpected benefits grew out of having key employees serve as presenters at some of the G4 educational sessions. Like Marlow, other G4 members were proud to learn that such talented people chose Rodale over better-known companies. Many of the cousins had heard of these employees in conversations with their parents, but never actually had met them. "It was good to finally put a face to those names," says Marlow. Several cousins expressed appreciation that such top-flight employees—an editor-in-chief or a vice president, for example—would take the time to sit down with a group of four to eight cousins and talk with them.

"Our major strengths are our employees and the knowledge that they have to share with us," says Shelbi. "We are getting an internal understanding of what our departments do, what our employees do and how our business runs. We're able to understand what an editor does versus what a publisher does. We're able to understand how a book is developed, how it's produced, how it's written, how it's distributed." Shelbi notes that the cousins grew up in four different families and four different households. The education program, she says, allows them all to sit in one room together and get the same information from an employee who's doing the actual job.

The G4s say they feel better prepared for ownership as a result of the program. Because he doesn't have a business background, Marlow says he has benefited particularly from sessions that provided information on financial planning. He better understands the stake that he and his G4 peers have in the company and how, as owners, they should conduct themselves around employees and other businesspeople. Maya says she appreciates the experience she is getting working with her cousins because the ability to work with relatives is a necessity in a family business whether you're an employee, an owner or both.

Because they are so young, many of the cousins have not yet made career choices. For some, the program offers insight into what it's like to work at Rodale, Inc., and helps them think through whether they should aim for a position in the family business.

Has the education program met the goal of bringing the cousins and siblings closer as adults? Shelbi and Maya think so. One key factor is that after most learning sessions, the G4s join one another for dinner. "We take the time to sit together as a cousin group . . . and just chat about what's happening in our lives," says Shelbi.

When they were younger, the G4s all lived in the same town, Emmaus, and enjoyed a close extended family. Now, many are off to college or jobs in other locations. Maya says that because of the education program, she sees her cousins more now than she would otherwise. Not only does the program help them maintain the family closeness they knew as children, but, she says, it helps them see that as adult owners of a family business, "we're all in this together."

MAJOR CHALLENGES

As mundane as it is, scheduling is the biggest problem. Trying to get a minimum of four cousins together at one time and in one location is difficult, as is trying to find a time and location suitable for an employee to speak. Reducing the frequency of meetings and having them during school breaks and the summer has helped, but scheduling, say Maya and Shelbi, is still tough.

Another challenge has been getting feedback from their cousins. They finally learned that if you want feedback, you have to ask for it. We tell you what they did in Chapter 8.

It is important to note that they are taking advantage of a window of time during which the cousins are living in somewhat close proximity and are somewhat available, as most are not yet married with families of their own. Different families will encounter different opportunities that they should jump on when they see them. A single opportunity doesn't have to last forever to be important and valuable.

Chapter 6

The Schmidts

Everything Is Education

"We are lifelong learners," Sarah Schmidt says of the people in her business-owning family. They never assume that they've mastered something, she explains. "There's always more to learn. I think that is a value that drives us."

Learning is indeed a major theme of the Schmidt family, and family education knits together its business, its foundation, and the family itself. The Schmidts own U.S. Oil Co., Inc., in Combined Locks, Wisconsin. The company began in the 1950s and today engages primarily in the marketing of petroleum products and the wholesale distribution of automotive parts and tires. It employs more than 1,000 people.

Family education and development are among the top priorities of Sarah Schmidt, president of the family board that was established in 2005. In her mid-30s, Sarah leads the five-member family board that governs the 90-plus U.S. Oil shareholders, including virtually everyone in the family, including in-laws. Sarah, who earned a doctorate in clinical psychology, is a member of the third generation and a current board member of the company.

Her role as family board president correlates with that of the president and CEO executive chairman of the business, with whom she works in partnership. As a sign of the great value of the family board to the family, Sarah and the five other family board members are paid. Small though it is, the family board reflects a diversity of which Sarah is proud. The board includes members of the third and fourth generations, a good balance of males and females, and both in-laws and direct-descendant family members. Ownership ranges from members with only a tiny percentage of the company to one person with an 8 percent stake.

EDUCATION: THE KEY TO COMMITTEES

The Schmidt family board has two committees, and education is the essence of each. The Social Responsibility Committee works collaboratively with the U.S. Oil/Schmidt Family Foundation, and one of this committee's most important charges is educating the shareholders about the work of the foundation. "Every time the members meet," says Sarah, "they educate themselves on one of the projects that the foundation has been involved with over time. So they bring in someone who is working in the orphanage in Mexico that we sponsor, or they bring in an individual who is leading work groups to Haiti . . . It's been a very cool experience to watch the members of the committee become very connected with causes that they really didn't know much about previously."

The company's founders began many of the family's philanthropic relationships, Sarah explains. Now the family has third- and fourth-generation shareholders who are very committed to their parents' and grandparents' philanthropies as a result of learning about them. Early in 2008, three family members set out for Nairobi, Kenya, to spend 10 days visiting a nearby community center built with foundation funds and contributions from individual family members.

"This has been a project we've been involved in for a very long time, partnering with a missionary priest . . . For the first time, shareholders [took] a look at it," says Sarah. On their return, the travelers reported at the annual shareholder meeting on what they learned about the center. "People will see their mom or cousin or sister-in-law in the photos," said Sarah. "I know it's going to change things. I think we'll have a very different sense of connection to the project itself."

Education and passionately held family values intersect in the work of the Social Responsibility Committee. Many of the Schmidts are Catholics, and the family has long been connected to missionary priests, sometimes in relationships dating back to high-school friendships that developed before a classmate chose the priesthood.

"A real uniqueness of our foundation is that we really try to help the world's poor, and that has taken us into different parts of the world," says Sarah. "It was very much an expression of the values of the three [business] founders. But now it's becoming an expression of the values of the whole shareholder group just by virtue of the fact that people are really learning about it and taking ownership."

The foundation gives away almost $1 million a year, not only to international projects but also to causes in the company's community. As the Social Responsibility Committee members learn more about the work of the foundation, the family board hopes to put procedures and structure in place so that family shareholders will have more of a voice in philanthropic initiatives or feel that they have a clearer way to participate.

The second committee of the family board, the Education and Leadership Development Committee, runs the annual shareholder meeting, which has some significant educational components. In addition, it implements periodic Learning Forums—short seminars on topics important to the shareholders. The committee also facilitates a company summer internship program for young shareholders. Details on the program follow below.

THE ANNUAL MEETING

"A huge education event" is how Sarah describes the annual shareholder meeting. "The whole day is really about information

sharing and getting feedback." Topics have ranged from communication skills and understanding family business to alternative
energy and the company's financial statement. Even the youngest shareholders—ages 4 to 17—have learning events geared to
them that might include education about community service,
team-building activities, or a tour of a new business.

LEARNING FORUMS

The Schmidts' learning forums offer an interim, briefer, and
more focused way for family shareholders to stay connected,
informed, and involved. For example, when U.S. Oil acquired
a sizable business, family members had a lot of questions about
the transaction: How did we do the deal? Why did we do it?
How is the integration going? What can we expect in the coming
year? The committee brought in the individuals who were running the business to give a presentation to the family and answer
questions.

"It was a great event because it was very brief. It's not the
daylong shareholder meeting. It's an hour, and then it's dinner
and cocktails," says Sarah. She notes the importance of the learning forums being social, too, because the family is now so large.
"Some people see each other all the time, but we certainly don't
interact as a family very often."

While family meetings in the past have included non-busi-
ness subjects such as communication issues, the learning forums
are focused on the company. They address family members as
shareholders and revolve around what is of concern to them.
"There may be a point at which we broaden ourselves beyond
that, but right now, there are so many topics that are very much
ownership related that are important. They are taking the front
burners," Sarah says.

The forums have included presentations on company divi-
sions, the price of fuel, and estate planning. The Education and
Leadership Development Committee is responsible for finding

the instructors. If a company division is the topic, the division head usually will make the presentation. If the subject is estate planning, the committee may choose one of the family's advisors or someone in the field who is not only knowledgeable but also can present the information well.

SHAREHOLDER INTERNSHIP PROGRAM

The Education and Leadership Development Committee facilitates a summer internship program for shareholders ages 16 to 24. The program's goals include providing the young people with meaningful work experience at U.S. Oil; exposing them to core company operations; enhancing their skill sets to help them obtain full-time employment after college; and building relationships among the third, fourth, and fifth generations of shareholders.

Family member Emily Schmidt served as the facilitator for the 2007 and 2008 internship program. Each year she worked with company human resources associates to match five young family members with appropriate full-time and part-time positions and identify a mentor from within the company for each intern. She also discussed the program's goals and expectations with each intern's supervisor and parent or guardian. She communicated with the mentors, who were expected to meet individually with their interns every other week and help them understand the company as well as how their skills and interests could translate into future employment. The mentors were also directed to provide feedback to Emily about the program.

In addition to getting on-the-job experience, the interns met as a group three times during the summer for learning seminars aimed at addressing their needs and interests. Social gatherings held after business hours were designed to build both relationships and a team mentality among the members of the fourth generation. Throughout the program, Emily maintained regular communication with each intern and was available for additional meetings with each supervisor, mentor or intern, as needed.

SCHMIDT FAMILY EDUCATION LOGISTICS

The family board's budget includes line items for meetings, forums and other educational expenses. Shareholders must approve the family board budget, as the funds actually come out of the company budget. The annual shareholder meeting is held in Wisconsin and expenses are covered for family members who must travel, if they decide to turn in their receipts. Travelers stay with local family members, so there are no hotel bills.

Learning forums are held twice a year. About 65 percent of the Schmidt family lives near the company's Wisconsin head-quarters, but the rest of the family is scattered across the country. The Education and Leadership Development Committee devised a way to accommodate both groups in the learning forums. Shareholders in or near Combined Locks attend in person and have dinner. Those who live far away receive an e-mailed copy of the presentation in advance and can call in with their questions during the forum. Even finding a way to accomplish that, with a good conference-call system, has involved a great deal of learning on the part of committee members.

TAKING ADVANTAGE OF EVERY
TEACHABLE MOMENT

"I feel like everything we do is about education," says Sarah. She offers this example: Suppose she is planning to write a letter to the shareholders about the need to fill some seats on the company board. "I'm going to take about a paragraph of that letter to remind them what the job of the board is, who's doing it, and what committees we have, because I know that everybody needs to hear it again.

"Now, I could just simply write a letter saying, 'Three terms have expired. Here's the slate. Here's your ballot. Return it in a week.' But I'd be missing out on an opportunity. So I feel like every time we interact with the shareholders, it's our job to be thinking about how we can provide or share some learning." She emphasizes the word "we" and says it's not just her job or the job of the family board committees to educate—it's the responsibility of everyone active in the shareholder group.

Another avenue of education is the shareholder website, which posts the company's monthly financials as well as quarterly updates from U.S. Oil's president and CEO and its executive chairman, and from the family president. In addition, all the members of the family board create updates for their areas of responsibility. Also included are all the family's policies and information about upcoming meetings. What has family education done for the Schmidts?

"It has brought us closer together," answers Sarah. "I think it has really helped our company become stronger and healthier." She points out that the business climate has become more complicated in recent years and the petroleum markets are more volatile. As a result, U.S. Oil has had to make a lot of tough decisions over the last decade. The more educated the family shareholders have been about business issues, the easier it has been to make those decisions, she observes. "There isn't a lot of time to mess around. So people need to be sharp. We need to be assets. And I think that family education has helped us become more of that."

Chapter 7

The Dean

Preserving a Family Legacy

What if an age-old family business is altered and the extended family's only connection is a family office? What would happen to the children? That's what worried May Johnson when it became clear that the third-generation brothers who owned the company she worked for were going to sell major parts of the business and strike out on their own with separate enterprises. But they funded a unique family office along with their sister, who had not been involved in the family business.

May Johnson is a very real person, although May Johnson is not her real name. However, the family she serves values its privacy for a variety of reasons, including security, and has asked that she and the family not be identified. In keeping with those wishes, we will refer to the family as "the family," to the family business as "the company," to the family office as "the family office," and to the family's foundation as "the family foundation." May's story is just too good and instructive not to be told. We are honored to tell it and appreciative to the family for letting us do so.

Like many older business-owning families, the family is a complicated one, complete with complex family dynamics that are so often prevalent in multigenerational family business. For 18 years, May worked as the executive assistant and manager of personal affairs for the second-generation owner/operator of the company and was with him during the transition of ownership to the two third-generation brothers. When he passed away, May recalls, the fourth generation consisted of "a group of kids from age 5 to 24 who were only sporadically together."

May asked for and was given the challenge of educating the members of the fourth generation on their participation in the company. "I felt that the knowledge of the business that I learned from their grandfather would be lost unless I became their guide," she said. The family agreed. She had, after all, been involved in the company's major 100th anniversary celebrations and was familiar with the corporate history. "I also had intimate knowledge of four generations of family members," she said. Most important, she had the family's trust.

She developed a leadership training program consisting of five-to-ten-week modules meant to teach the participants about the business's operating companies and parent company as well as the family foundation and the then-existing family office. This was a collaborative effort with other non-family company employees along with outside consultants. Young family members could sign up during their semester breaks for the modules, which were largely internships and hands-on training that covered

- A hard work experience, such as driving a dump truck
- A team experience in the field, such as being part of the manager's team in a personnel office or engineering group
- A head office experience in each of the company's operations
- A five-week stint at the family foundation, including training for sitting on its board of directors
- A work experience in the marketing department of each of the operating companies, in the legal department of the parent company, in the existing family office and in the business's history center
- A work experience outside the company

The program also provided a shared experience for the fourth-generation members and taught them to appreciate their heritage and the work in which the previous generations had been engaged.

A MAJOR SHIFT

"The sale of the company put the kibosh on the program for a time because the arena had changed," says May. "Gone were the operating companies in which the modules played out."

The succeeding arena in which May could operate was a new family office launched in the late 1990s. It differs from other family offices in that it has no business assets. It looks after some of the family's joint interests, including its archives; the family foundation; trust administration for family members; education for the next-generation members and their spouses; and social events that the brothers' companies combine, such as service recognition and an annual golf tournament.

On advice from a family business consultant, the family endowed its foundation and challenged the fourth generation to take it over. So began a three-year succession plan for the family foundation, which has since been successfully transferred to the members of the fourth generation.

"This endeavor has turned out to be a great source of education," May says. "They had to develop their own governance for the family foundation, including choosing and setting up a board of directors, selecting investment managers for the fund, developing a policy manual for grant making, designing and implementing a website, and so on. Throughout the process, I was lucky to be their shepherdess and to facilitate their many meetings."

In addition to serving as general manager and corporate secretary of the family office, May is secretary of the family foundation and attends all its board meetings. "I am happy to report that these young people are diligent in their review of grant applications and strategic in their giving. They have changed the family foundation, which began in 1965, from having a reactive to a proactive approach in philanthropy, and they have totally professionalized it."

She also observes that the fourth-generation members hold close to their hearts the values of their grandparents, such as hard work, integrity, teamwork, and respect for and loyalty to employees.

May's role as an educator of the younger generation continues under the aegis of the family office. Its budget enables young family members to attend conferences and seminars where they can learn more about family business and philanthropy. She has helped many of the fourth generation with their education choices and career planning, and has seen to it that they learn about trusts, wills and estates, prenuptial agreements, and cohabitation agreements for family members who choose to live with someone without getting married.

The family office arranges for family meetings at which members learn about topics such as family business in general and mission and vision statements, and get updates on the third-generation brothers' businesses and the family foundation. There is also a family council that includes educational components at its meetings, as well as a retreat when required just for the members of the fourth generation.

In 2005, the family office arranged for a contingent of the fourth generation to travel extensively throughout China for four-and-a-half months, accompanied by experts on China and a translator. The young people "were sent as ambassadors of their family's businesses and were responsible for sending weekly reports to everyone," May says. "On their return, they presented many times to all the different boards of directors at their parents' businesses as well as to one or two outside groups. This was an exceptional team-building experience and it forced them into a very different and challenging arena."

FAR-REACHING EFFECTS

In reflecting on the education effort that she initiated, May wanted to help the young people understand what their fathers and mothers were doing, in terms of business and philanthropy and what opportunities that might hold for them.

Over the years, education has had some far-reaching effects. It has brought the G4 members, friends to begin with, even closer together and enabled them to function effectively as a team. It has brought the members of the third generation closer to their children. The parents observed the next generation in operation during the business training programs and during the family foundation's succession process. Communication between the two generations not only increased, but the parents saw their children, nieces, and nephews in a new light. The education program, May says, "did a great deal to educate the parents about their own kids." The succession process also resulted in teamwork among the not-so-close third generation. The two generations wrote a series of letters back and forth, with the third generation coming together as a unified voice to tell the G4s what it wanted, and the G4s getting together and making their own unified response.

May's experience underscores the importance of having a dean who is dedicated to the family members that he or she serves and someone who they can trust. She says she "never EVER" reported to the parents on what the G4s were doing. "I was the kids' confidante, and they knew that." The G4s knew she was in their corner, but it was the parents who paid her salary. "So that's a huge gift that the parents gave their kids," says May.

PART III

THE FINISHING TOUCHES

Details matter, but if you have never done something before, it's hard to know what those details are. If you are initiating family education, however, you can benefit from the experiences of others. By doing so, you will avoid some mistakes and add polish to your program.

Chapter 8

Making Your Program a Success

It may be easier than you think to make your family education program a hit. Sometimes, business-owning families try too hard when a simpler approach would produce a better result. Based on our experience in working with families, there are certain success factors that go into creating family education programs that are both appealing and effective.

- **Start modestly, and build as you get more experience.** Or as Shelbi R. Gourniak of the Rodale family puts it, "Don't do too much too quickly." She says that in devising the family's fourth-generation education program, she and her cousin, Maya Rodale, tried to hold too many sessions in too short a period of time. "It just became too challenging for the family members to physically get to these sessions," she says. By making the program a challenge to attend, it became more like work, defeating the purpose of it being fun and exciting as well as educational.
- **Leave people wanting more.** Avoid being too complex and overwhelming people. Aim to have people leave a meeting saying that it should have been longer. You don't want them to feel inundated but rather that the topic needed to be discussed in greater depth. You can achieve this by doing the following.

◆ **Be concrete, meaty, and tangible, especially with the next generation.** Members of the next generation tend to be impatient with "touchy-feely, getting-to-know-you" approaches. They like facts and figures and can tell if what's being presented is just fluff. They want to really get to the heart of things.

◆ **Involve people as much as possible and make your program as active as you can.** If you can do education on site, do so. Visit places so that people can see what you're teaching about. If you can't visit the location, use pictures or videos. Bring the subject into the room. Make it immediate. Think of the Schmidt family members' first-ever visit to a family-sponsored community center in Kenya and the stories and pictures they brought back.

Also, get people involved in planning and delivering education, if you can—especially when the program is for young people. If they know that one of their peers planned it, they'll be kinder. But if they think their parents planned it, they'll probably be more critical.

Sometimes, older family members say, "Our young people need these topics, and here's how we're going to teach it to them. Hold on tight!" Instead, it's more effective to engage the members of your target audience in the selection of topics and in the design and process of the type of education. Resist the temptation to cram too much in too short a period of time.

◆ **Leverage existing information.** That is, make use of whatever already exists. For example, many companies inform employees on a regular basis how the business is doing. Make what the employees receive available to family members. Does your company provide a strategic planning update to top management on a regular basis? Family can be included, too. Some companies invite family members to sit in on orientation for new employees as a way to learn about the business.

Make sure that family members are on the mailing lists of the company publications. As simple as that is, family firms sometimes neglect to do that. Think about what is already going out to customers, employees, or suppliers that the family and owners might also find interesting. Another tip is to emulate Sarah Schmidt, who uses every communication to include an educational point or two.

By leveraging existing information, you are making good use of your resources. We hate to see families spend a lot of time and money developing materials specifically for themselves when there's already a lot available that families can customize to their own needs.

◆ **Plan for the near term.** Don't plan beyond one-and-a-half or two years, because things change so quickly that you'll just squander your time. We've seen families spend months and months putting a curriculum together, only to discover that things are changing so rapidly or so many unforeseen events have occurred that their programs are out of date before they have even begun.

◆ **Give your program the right resources.** Get qualified people to help you with it and provide an adequate budget for it. Don't think of it as just an *exercise;* think of it as a *program* and an *investment* more than a cost.

◆ **Repeat topics as necessary.** A curriculum is not a checklist. You can't say, "Oh, we did that in 2002," and then think you're finished with it or the family no longer needs it. A number of topics need revisiting because the family is growing and changing or new people join as spouses. In addition, some topics need review and reinforcement. We see families that do communication skills workshops every single year to refine and hone those skills and remind people what good communication is all about. As Sarah Schmidt points out, most family members "don't live and breathe this stuff every day," and retention is an issue.

EXHIBIT 6   **Five Topics Worth Repeating**

1. Estate planning
2. How to read a financial statement
3. Communication skills
4. Shareholder dividend and redemption policy issues
5. Tax planning strategies

- **Make it fun.** Aim for a good mix of topics and teaching methods. More than most groups, families need experiential education. Instead of lecture-type education, use cases, games, and hands-on learning. Think in terms of Outward Bound or Junior Achievement instead of a classroom, and enable family members to learn by doing, engaging and practicing.
- **Get continuous feedback.** Solicit people's evaluations all the time. If she had it to do over, says Maya Rodale, "I would start getting more feedback from the get-go." Initially, the Rodales' attempt to get feedback was somewhat haphazard. Finally, after their education program was about 18 months old, Maya and Shelbi developed the survey below and began to receive valuable information.

The Rodales and others suggest asking family members to write down what's working and what's not, what they'd like more of, and what suggestions they have. Feedback is really useful, and getting it is one of the reasons you don't want to plan too far in advance. Instead, you want to be able to take what you're learning along the way as planners and adjust to what your audience wants and needs. "Success depends on everyone's participation," says Maya. "So getting people involved and getting them involved in a way they're satisfied with is essential." Feedback provides a way.

Here is the feedback tool that the Rodales came up with. Remember that Rodale, Inc., publishes magazines and books and notice how the survey reflects the business in which the company is engaged.

EXHIBIT 7   **Rodale G4 Education Survey**

What have you thought about the education sessions so far?
   Super
   Fine
   Boring

Do you want us to continue offering education sessions?
    Yes
    No

Do you prefer meeting in NY or PA?
    NY
    PA

How many times per year would you be able to attend sessions?
    0
    1–2
    3–4
    5–6
    More than 6

What times would be best for you if we were to organize more sessions?
    Fridays
    Summer
    Other

I would like to come to more sessions taught by:
    Our staff
    Other magazine or book people
    Our family business consultant

Are you interested in learning more about business finances?
    Yes
    No

Personal finances?
    Yes
    No

Are there any topics you want to learn about that we haven't offered yet?
    Books
    Magazines

Continued

Online
Marketing
Circulation
Production/Printing
Institute
Finance
Budgeting
Photos/Imaging
Philanthropy
Other:

Do you want us to organize a G4 meal after sessions?
Yes
No

Do you want to take a field trip?
Yes
No
Distribution center
Prevention press facility
Other:

Is there anything you think should be included in the next annual budget?
Travel
Education
G4 meals

An even simpler evaluation form would ask the following:

1. What was the most important accomplishment of the meeting? Why?
2. What were the most valuable aspects of the meeting? How can we make sure they are part of future meetings?
3. What aspects of the meeting could be improved? How?
4. What important follow-up remains ahead?
5. Other comments:

ADVICE FROM THE FAMILIES

Based on their experience in creating and implementing a family education program, the Rodale cousins offer this advice to others embarking on a similar effort:

- **Be patient.** "It does take time to get these [programs] together, and it takes a lot of effort to juggle all those schedules and needs and interests," says Maya.

- **Know your audience.** Get an idea of who wants to learn what and what backgrounds they have. Try to start your sessions so that everybody's on an equal playing field, and then build up to get everybody educated to the same level.

- **Get engaging speakers.** The most knowledgeable person might not be the best person to speak to a particular group, warns Shelbi. She suggests looking for someone who can educate your group in the most effective way. For the Rodales, Shelbi says, that has meant finding people who are eager to talk to a "group of 20-somethings and who can present the material in a way that the 20-somethings get it and get excited about it."

- **Make a record.** Keep a binder with notes on every education session. When people are absent, they can look through the notes later to catch up on major points and see what the handouts were.

- **Tailor your method of communication to each individual instead of trying to make people conform to your style.** Some people won't respond to e-mail at all or may not respond to group e-mail, so you have to target them personally. Some people respond best to text messages, while others want a telephone call. In the beginning, it's smart to ask, "What's the best way to contact you?"

Sarah Schmidt also has some advice:

- **Keep it simple.** When you're starting out, she suggests, "Pick one or two things that the group would like to know a bit more about, and get together for an hour." She has seen a number of families make the process very complicated, and when it becomes too complicated, she notes, "it gives you a reason not to do it."

◆ **Expect to learn as you go.** "There are lots of things we could have done differently, but there was a lot of learning along the way," says Sarah. She sees developing an education program as an evolutionary, fluid process. "Once you start and you have some success with your program, it becomes easier and easier," she adds.

EXHIBIT 8   **The 12 Factors that Make Education a Success**

1. Start modestly, and keep things simple.
2. Leave people wanting more.
3. Be concrete and meaty with the next generation.
4. Involve members of your target audience in planning and delivery.
5. Leverage existing information.
6. Plan for the near term.
7. Provide the right resources.
8. Revisit topics as necessary.
9. Make your sessions fun.
10. Get continuous feedback.
11. Know your audience and get the best speakers for your particular group.
12. Learn as you go.

Chapter 9

Summary

The benefits of family education to a family and its business are virtually incalculable. Who can gauge what "closeness" is when learning together brings family members closer, enhancing friendships and building understanding and respect for one another? How do we measure the contribution that family shareholders make when they have educated themselves about their business and joined together in making good decisions on its behalf? Who can put a price on the joy and excitement that grandparents feel when the youngest generation begins to recognize, respect, and take pride in what their forebears have accomplished in building and preserving a family business? How can one calculate the satisfaction that parents experience when their adult children assume the stewardship of their family's firm?

Although we can't measure the value of family education, we do know that business-owning families thrive when they create and implement learning programs for family members. Time and time again, we have seen that such learning

- Prepares family members for effective management, governance, and ownership
- Enhances team building, enabling family members to make good decisions as a group
- Makes all family members feel valued and appreciated, whether or not they work in the business

- Serves as the core or glue of the family as it becomes larger and more diverse
- Preserves the family's legacy and values

From this book, you have learned that family education is most effective when it is designed by the family to meet its own distinctive needs. You saw how the fourth-generation Rodale family members initiated an education program just for their generation because they wanted to learn more about the company founded by their great-grandfather and to prepare themselves for their roles as owners. Their program is quite informal, but it meets the needs of the members of this mostly 20-something group, many of whom are still in college.

You observed how the Schmidts instituted a more rigorous, formal approach, planned and overseen by committees of the family board. Because virtually every family member is an owner, the emphasis has been on shareholder education, including learning about the business and about the family's foundation.

You also found out how one highly respected non-family employee, May Johnson, saw a vital need for education for the next generation in a business-owning family. With the blessing of that family, she launched a program that initially was intended to prepare the young people for roles in the business. When the business was sold, however, May revamped the program. It now provides education aimed at preserving the history and legacy of the family and its original business, preparing the young people for potential roles in the family's foundation, and teaching wise investing.

As these stories illustrate, each family's education program is unique, just as yours will be. To be effective, family education must take into consideration a number of factors, including the family's values, the nature of the business and the industry it occupies, the size and ages of the family, and the desires of family members.

This book has provided you with many tools and tips to help you plan and implement your own program. You have read about some ideas for the kinds of topics that can be covered. You have learned how other families fund their programs, get feedback and use every possible means (newsletters, family meetings, websites, internships, shareholder meetings) to support and reinforce education.

What's important now is to get started. Most families learn as they go and get outside assistance when they need it. It will help to remember the advice we offered earlier: start modestly, and build as you get more experience.

So start. Just start. The sooner you do, the sooner your family and your family enterprise can experience the power of and enjoy the benefits of family education.

Resources

Information and Referrals

Family Firm Institute, 200 Lincoln Street #201, Boston, Massachusetts 02111; 617-482-3045 or www.ffi.org. An organization of family business professionals, FFI can provide information on speakers as well as university-based family business programs.

The Family Business Consulting Group, Inc., 1220-B Kennesaw Circle, Marietta, Georgia 30066; 888-421-0110 or http://www.efamilybusiness.com.

Family Business Education

Canadian Association of Family Enterprise, 1388 C Cornwall Road, Oakville, Ontario, Canada L6J7W5; 1-866-849-0099; http://www.cafecanada.ca/programs.cfm.

Council on Foundations, 2121 Crystal Drive, Suite 700, Arlington, VA 22202; 800-673-9036; http://www.cof.org. A good source of education on family foundations and philanthropy.

The Family Business Consulting Group, Inc. (see above).

Family Business Network, 23 Chemin de Bellerive, P.O. Box 915, 1001 Lausanne, Switzerland; 41 21 618 0223 or http://www.fbn-i.org. An international organization of business-owning families, FBN conducts educational programs in a variety of countries.

Family Office Exchange, 100 S. Wacker Drive, Suite 900, Chicago, Illinois 60606; 312-327-1200; http://www.foxexchange .com. Specializes in education about family offices and wealth.

INSEAD, Boulevard de Constance, Fontainebleau, Cedex 77305, France; 33 16 072 40 00; http://www.insead.edu/executives/fame .cfm.

Loedstar S.A., 72 Boulevard de Saint-Georges, 1205 Geneva, Switzerland; 41 22 328 4610; http://www.loedstar.com.

Leadership Education

Center for Creative Leadership, P.O. Box 26300, Greensboro, North Carolina 27438-6300; 336-545-2810; http://www.ccl.org.

Next Generation Leadership Institute, Loyola University Chicago Family Business Center, 1 E. Pearson, Suite 314, Chicago, Illinois 60611; 312-915-6490; www.luc.edu/fbc.

Index

The Authors

Amy M. Schuman is a Principal Consultant of the Family Business Consulting Group, Inc., and works with family businesses on leadership development, communication skills, and team building. Amy was the founding facilitator of the Next Generation Leadership Institute, an intensive, two-year program for next-generation family business leaders that is part of the Loyola University Chicago Family Business Center.

John L. Ward is Co-founder of the Family Business Consulting Group, Inc. He is Clinical Professor at the Kellogg School of Management and teaches strategic management, business leadership, and family enterprise continuity.

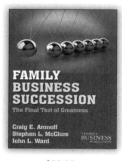

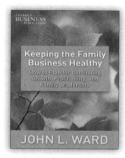
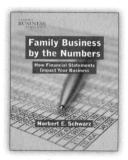